WORK

Cor

Nearly 6.5 million p
ly 252,000 construction sites across the nation on any given day. The fatal injury rate for the construction industry is higher than the national average in this category for all industries.

Potential hazards for workers in construction include:

- Falls (from heights);
- Trench collapse;
- Scaffold collapse;
- Electric shock and arc flash/arc blast;
- Failure to use proper personal protective equipment; and
- Repetitive motion injuries.

Occupational Safety and Health Administration
U.S. Department of Labor
www.osha.gov

CONSTRUCTION

Hazards & Solutions

For construction, the 10 OSHA standards most frequently included in the agency's citations in FY 2004 were:

1. Scaffolding
2. Fall protection (scope, application, definitions)
3. Excavations (general requirements)
4. Ladders
5. Head protection
6. Excavations (requirements for protective systems)
7. Hazard communication
8. Fall protection (training requirements)
9. Construction (general safety and health provisions)
10. Electrical (wiring methods, design and protection)

OSHA
Occupational Safety and
Health Administration

WORKER SAFETY SERIES

Scaffolding

Hazard: When scaffolds are not erected or used properly, fall hazards can occur. About 2.3 million construction workers frequently work on scaffolds. Protecting these workers from scaffold-related accidents would prevent an estimated 4,500 injuries and 50 fatalities each year.

Solutions:

- Scaffold must be sound, rigid and sufficient to carry its own weight plus four times the maximum intended load without settling or displacement. It must be erected on solid footing.
- Unstable objects, such as barrels, boxes, loose bricks or concrete blocks must not be used to support scaffolds or planks.
- Scaffold must not be erected, moved, dismantled or altered except under the supervision of a competent person.
- Scaffold must be equipped with guardrails, midrails and toeboards.
- Scaffold accessories such as braces, brackets, trusses, screw legs or ladders that are damaged or weakened from any cause must be immediately repaired or replaced.
- Scaffold platforms must be tightly planked with scaffold plank grade material or equivalent.
- A "competent person" must inspect the scaffolding and, at designated intervals, reinspect it.
- Rigging on suspension scaffolds must be inspected by a competent person before each shift and after any occurrence that could affect structural integrity to ensure that all connections are tight and that no

Occupational Safety and
Health Administration

damage to the rigging has occurred since its last use.

- Synthetic and natural rope used in suspension scaffolding must be protected from heat-producing sources.
- Employees must be instructed about the hazards of using diagonal braces as fall protection.
- Scaffold can be accessed by using ladders and stairwells.
- Scaffolds must be at least 10 feet from electric power lines at all times.

Occupational Safety and Health Administration

Fall Protection

Hazard: Each year, falls consistently account for the greatest number of fatalities in the construction industry. A number of factors are often involved in falls, including unstable working surfaces, misuse or failure to use fall protection equipment and human error. Studies have shown that using guardrails, fall arrest systems, safety nets, covers and restraint systems can prevent many deaths and injuries from falls.

Solutions:
- Consider using aerial lifts or elevated platforms to provide safer elevated working surfaces;
- Erect guardrail systems with toeboards and warning lines or install control line systems to protect workers near the edges of floors and roofs;
- Cover floor holes; and/or
- Use safety net systems or personal fall arrest systems (body harnesses).

OSHA
Occupational Safety and Health Administration

CONSTRUCTION

Ladders

Hazard: Ladders and stairways are another source of injuries and fatalities among construction workers. OSHA estimates that there are 24,882 injuries and as many as 36 fatalities per year due to falls on stairways and ladders used in construction. Nearly half of these injuries were serious enough to require time off the job.

Solutions:

- Use the correct ladder for the task.
- Have a competent person visually inspect a ladder before use for any defects such as:
  - Structural damage, split/bent side rails, broken or missing rungs/steps/cleats and missing or damaged safety devices;
  - Grease, dirt or other contaminants that could cause slips or falls;
  - Paint or stickers (except warning labels) that could hide possible defects.
- Make sure that ladders are long enough to safely reach the work area.
- Mark or tag ("Do Not Use") damaged or defective ladders for repair or replacement, or destroy them immediately.
- Never load ladders beyond the maximum intended load or beyond the manufacturer's rated capacity.
- Be sure the load rating can support the weight of the user, including materials and tools.
- Avoid using ladders with metallic components near electrical work and overhead power lines.

Stairways

Hazard: Slips, trips and falls on stairways are a major source of injuries and fatalities among construction workers.

Solutions:
- Stairway treads and walkways must be free of dangerous objects, debris and materials.
- Slippery conditions on stairways and walkways must be corrected immediately.
- Make sure that treads cover the entire step and landing.
- Stairways having four or more risers or rising more than 30 inches must have at least one handrail.

OSHA
Occupational Safety and Health Administration

CONSTRUCTION

Trenching

Hazard: Trench collapses cause dozens of fatalities and hundreds of injuries each year. Trenching deaths rose in 2003.

Solutions:

- Never enter an unprotected trench.
- Always use a protective system for trenches 5 feet deep or greater.
- Employ a registered professional engineer to design a protective system for trenches 20 feet deep or greater.
- Protective Systems:
    - Sloping to protect workers by cutting back the trench wall at an angle inclined away from the excavation not steeper than a height/depth ratio of $1\frac{1}{2}$:1, according to the sloping requirements for the type of soil.

SLOPING. Maximum allowable slopes for excavations less than 20 ft. (6.09 m) based on soil type and angle to the horizontal are as follows:

TABLE V:2-1. ALLOWABLE SLOPES

Soil type	Height/Depth ratio	Slope angle
Stable Rock (granite or sandstone)	Vertical	90°
Type A (clay)	$\frac{3}{4}$:1	53°
Type B (gravel, silt)	1:1	45°
Type C (sand)	$1\frac{1}{2}$:1	34°
Type A (short-term)	$\frac{1}{2}$:1	63°
(For a maximum excavation depth of 12 ft.)		

Source: OSHA Technical Manual, Section V, Chap. 2, Excavations: Hazard Recognition in Trenching and Shoring (Jan. 1999).

Occupational Safety and Health Administration

- Shoring to protect workers by installing supports to prevent soil movement for trenches that do not exceed 20 feet in depth.
- Shielding to protect workers by using trench boxes or other types of supports to prevent soil cave-ins.

- Always provide a way to exit a trench--such as a ladder, stairway or ramp--no more than 25 feet of lateral travel for employees in the trench.
- Keep spoils at least two feet back from the edge of a trench.
- Make sure that trenches are inspected by a competent person prior to entry and after any hazard-increasing event such as a rainstorm, vibrations or excessive surcharge loads.

OSHA
Occupational Safety and
Health Administration

CONSTRUCTION

Cranes

Hazard: Significant and serious injuries may occur if cranes are not inspected before use and if they are not used properly. Often these injuries occur when a worker is struck by an overhead load or caught within the crane's swing radius. Many crane fatalities occur when the boom of a crane or its load line contact an overhead power line.

Solutions:

- Check all crane controls to insure proper operation before use.
- Inspect wire rope, chains and hook for any damage.
- Know the weight of the load that the crane is to lift.
- Ensure that the load does not exceed the crane's rated capacity.
- Raise the load a few inches to verify balance and the effectiveness of the brake system.
- Check all rigging prior to use; do not wrap hoist ropes or chains around the load.
- Fully extend outriggers.
- Do not move a load over workers.
- Barricade accessible areas within the crane's swing radius.
- Watch for overhead electrical distribution and transmission lines and maintain a safe working clearance of at least 10 feet from energized electrical lines.

Occupational Safety and Health Administration

Hazard Communication

Hazard: Failure to recognize the hazards associated with chemicals can cause chemical burns, respiratory problems, fires and explosions.

Solutions:

- Maintain a Material Safety Data Sheet (MSDS) for each chemical in the facility.
- Make this information accessible to employees at all times in a language or formats that are clearly understood by all affected personnel.
- Train employees on how to read and use the MSDS.
- Follow manufacturer's MSDS instructions for handling hazardous chemicals.
- Train employees about the risks of each hazardous chemical being used.
- Provide spill clean-up kits in areas where chemicals are stored.
- Have a written spill control plan.
- Train employees to clean up spills, protect themselves and properly dispose of used materials.
- Provide proper personal protective equipment and enforce its use.
- Store chemicals safely and securely.

OSHA
Occupational Safety and
Health Administration

CONSTRUCTION

Forklifts

Hazard: Approximately 100 employees are fatally injured and approximately 95,000 employees are injured every year while operating powered industrial trucks. Forklift turnover accounts for a significant number of these fatalities.

Solutions:

- Train and certify all operators to ensure that they operate forklifts safely.
- Do not allow any employee under 18 years old to operate a forklift.
- Properly maintain haulage equipment, including tires.
- Do not modify or make attachments that affect the capacity and safe operation of the forklift without written approval from the forklift's manufacturer.
- Examine forklift truck for defects before using.
- Follow safe operating procedures for picking up, moving, putting down and stacking loads.

OSHA
Occupational Safety and
Health Administration

WORKER SAFETY SERIES

- Drive safely--never exceed 5 mph and slow down in congested or slippery surface areas.
- Prohibit stunt driving and horseplay.
- Do not handle loads that are heavier than the capacity of the industrial truck.
- Remove unsafe or defective forklift trucks from service.
- Operators shall always wear seatbelts.
- Avoid traveling with elevated loads.
- Assure that rollover protective structure is in place.
- Make certain that the reverse signal alarm is operational and audible above the surrounding noise level.

Head Protection

Hazard: Serious head injuries can result from blows to the head.

Solution:
- Be sure that workers wear hard hats where there is a potential for objects falling from above, bumps to their heads from fixed objects, or accidental head contact with electrical hazards.

OSHA
Occupational Safety and Health Administration

Safety Checklists

The following checklists may help you take steps to avoid hazards that cause injuries, illnesses and fatalities. As always, be cautious and seek help if you are concerned about a potential hazard.

Personal Protective Equipment (PPE)

Eye and Face Protection

☐ Safety glasses or face shields are worn anytime work operations can cause foreign objects getting into the eye such as during welding, cutting, grinding, nailing (or when working with concrete and/or harmful chemicals or when exposed to flying particles).

☐ Eye and face protectors are selected based on anticipated hazards.

☐ Safety glasses or face shields are worn when exposed to any electrical hazards including work on energized electrical systems.

Foot Protection

☐ Construction workers should wear work shoes or boots with slip-resistant and puncture-resistant soles.

☐ Safety-toed footwear is worn to prevent crushed toes when working around heavy equipment or falling objects.

Hand Protection

☐ Gloves should fit snugly.

☐ Workers wear the right gloves for the job (for example, heavy-duty rubber gloves for concrete work, welding gloves for welding, insulated gloves and sleeves when exposed to electrical hazards).

Head Protection

☐ Workers shall wear hard hats where there is a potential for objects falling from above, bumps to their heads from fixed objects, or of accidental head contact with electrical hazards.

☐ Hard hats are routinely inspected for dents, cracks or deterioration.

☐ Hard hats are replaced after a heavy blow or electrical shock.

☐ Hard hats are maintained in good condition.

Scaffolding

☐ Scaffolds should be set on sound footing.

☐ Damaged parts that affect the strength of the scaffold are taken out of service.

☐ Scaffolds are not altered.

☐ All scaffolds should be fully planked.

☐ Scaffolds are not moved horizontally while workers are on them unless they are designed to be mobile and workers have been trained in the proper procedures.

☐ Employees are not permitted to work on scaffolds when covered with snow, ice, or other slippery materials.

☐ Scaffolds are not erected or moved within 10 feet of power lines.

☐ Employees are not permitted to work on scaffolds in bad weather or high winds

OSHA
Occupational Safety and
Health Administration

CONSTRUCTION

unless a competent person has determined that it is safe to do so.

☐ Ladders, boxes, barrels, buckets or other makeshift platforms are not used to raise work height.

☐ Extra material is not allowed to build up on scaffold platforms.

☐ Scaffolds should not be loaded with more weight than they were designed to support.

Electrical Safety

☐ Work on new and existing energized (hot) electrical circuits is prohibited until all power is shut off and grounds are attached.

☐ An effective Lockout/Tagout system is in place.

☐ Frayed, damaged or worn electrical cords or cables are promptly replaced.

☐ All extension cords have grounding prongs.

☐ Protect flexible cords and cables from damage. Sharp corners and projections should be avoided.

☐ Use extension cord sets used with portable electric tools and appliances that are the three-wire type and designed for hard or extra-hard service. (Look for some of the following letters imprinted on the casing: S, ST, SO, STO.)

☐ All electrical tools and equipment are maintained in safe condition and checked regularly for defects and taken out of service if a defect is found.

☐ Do not bypass any protective system or device designed to protect employees from contact with electrical energy.

OSHA
Occupational Safety and Health Administration

- [ ] Overhead electrical power lines are located and identified.
- [ ] Ensure that ladders, scaffolds, equipment or materials never come within 10 feet of electrical power lines.
- [ ] All electrical tools must be properly grounded unless they are of the double insulated type.
- [ ] Multiple plug adapters are prohibited.

Floor and Wall Openings

- [ ] Floor openings (12 inches or more) are guarded by a secured cover, a guardrail or equivalent on all sides (except at entrances to stairways).
- [ ] Toeboards are installed around the edges of permanent floor openings (where persons may pass below the opening).

Elevated Surfaces

- [ ] Signs are posted, when appropriate, showing the elevated surface load capacity.
- [ ] Surfaces elevated more than 48 inches above the floor or ground have standard guardrails.
- [ ] All elevated surfaces (beneath which people or machinery could be exposed to falling objects) have standard 4-inch toeboards.
- [ ] A permanent means of entry and exit with handrails is provided to elevated storage and work surfaces.
- [ ] Material is piled, stacked or racked in a way that prevents it from tipping, falling, collapsing, rolling or spreading.

Occupational Safety and Health Administration

Hazard Communication

- [ ] A list of hazardous substances used in the workplace is maintained and readily available at the worksite.
- [ ] There is a written hazard communication program addressing Material Safety Data Sheets (MSDS), labeling and employee training.
- [ ] Each container of a hazardous substance (vats, bottles, storage tanks) is labeled with product identity and a hazard warning(s) (communicating the specific health hazards and physical hazards).
- [ ] Material Safety Data Sheets are readily available at all times for each hazardous substance used.
- [ ] There is an effective employee training program for hazardous substances.

Crane Safety

- [ ] Cranes and derricks are restricted from operating within 10 feet of any electrical power line.
- [ ] The upper rotating structure supporting the boom and materials being handled is provided with an electrical ground while working near energized transmitter towers.
- [ ] Rated load capacities, operating speed and instructions are posted and visible to the operator.
- [ ] Cranes are equipped with a load chart.
- [ ] The operator understands and uses the load chart.
- [ ] The operator can determine the angle and length of the crane boom at all times.

- [ ] Crane machinery and other rigging equipment is inspected daily prior to use to make sure that it is in good condition.
- [ ] Accessible areas within the crane's swing radius are barricaded.
- [ ] Tag lines are used to prevent dangerous swing or spin of materials when raised or lowered by a crane or derrick.
- [ ] Illustrations of hand signals to crane and derrick operators are posted on the job site.
- [ ] The signal person uses correct signals for the crane operator to follow.
- [ ] Crane outriggers are extended when required.
- [ ] Crane platforms and walkways have anti-skid surfaces.
- [ ] Broken, worn or damaged wire rope is removed from service.
- [ ] Guardrails, hand holds and steps are provided for safe and easy access to and from all areas of the crane.
- [ ] Load testing reports/certifications are available.
- [ ] Tower crane mast bolts are properly torqued to the manufacturer's specifications.
- [ ] Overload limits are tested and correctly set.
- [ ] The maximum acceptable load and the last test results are posted on the crane.
- [ ] Initial and annual inspections of all hoisting and rigging equipment are performed and reports are maintained.
- [ ] Only properly trained and qualified operators are allowed to work with hoisting and rigging equipment.

Forklifts

- [ ] Forklift truck operators are competent to operate these vehicles safely as demonstrated by their successful completion of training and evaluation.
- [ ] No employee under 18 years old is allowed to operate a forklift.
- [ ] Forklifts are inspected daily for proper condition of brakes, horns, steering, forks and tires.
- [ ] Powered industrial trucks (forklifts) meet the design and construction requirements established in American National Standards Institute (ANSI) for Powered Industrial Trucks, Part II ANSI B56.1-1969.
- [ ] Written approval from the truck manufacturer is obtained for any modification or additions which affect capacity and safe operation of the vehicle.
- [ ] Capacity, operation and maintenance instruction plates, tags or decals are changed to indicate any modifications or additions to the vehicle.
- [ ] Battery charging is conducted in areas specifically designated for that purpose.
- [ ] Material handling equipment is provided for handling batteries, including conveyors, overhead hoists or equivalent devices.
- [ ] Reinstalled batteries are properly positioned and secured in the truck.
- [ ] Smoking is prohibited in battery charging areas.
- [ ] Precautions are taken to prevent open flames, sparks or electric arcs in battery charging areas.
- [ ] Refresher training is provided and an evaluation is conducted whenever a fork-

OSHA
Occupational Safety and
Health Administration

lift operator has been observed operating the vehicle in an unsafe manner and when an operator is assigned to drive a different type of truck.

- [ ] Load and forks are fully lowered, controls neutralized, power shut off and brakes set when a powered industrial truck is left unattended.
- [ ] There is sufficient headroom for the forklift and operator under overhead installations, lights, pipes, sprinkler systems, etc.
- [ ] Overhead guards are in place to protect the operator against falling objects.
- [ ] Trucks are operated at a safe speed.
- [ ] All loads are kept stable, safely arranged and fit within the rated capacity of the truck.
- [ ] Unsafe and defective trucks are removed from service.

OSHA
Occupational Safety and Health Administration

Construction Safety & Health Resources

Most resource materials can be found on the OSHA website: www.osha.gov

Publications

Publications can be downloaded or ordered at:
http://www.osha.gov/pls/publications/pubindex.list

A Guide to Scaffold Use in the Construction Industry
OSHA Publication 3150 (Revised 2002), 2.1 MB PDF, 73 pages.
Booklet in question-and-answer format highlights information about scaffold safety.
http://www.osha.gov/Publications/osha3150.pdf

Concrete and Masonry Construction
OSHA Publication 3106 (Revised 1998), 414 KB PDF, 32 pages.
Details information on OSHA's Concrete and Masonry standard.
http://www.osha.gov/Publications/osha3106.pdf

Crystalline Silica Exposure Card for Construction
OSHA Publication 3177 (Revised 2002), 2 pages.
Discusses silica hazards, and what employers and employees can do to protect against exposures to silica.
A Spanish version is also available. OSHA Publication 3179 (Revised 2003), 2 pages.

Excavations
OSHA Publication 2226 (Revised 2002), 533 KB PDF, 44 pages.
A detailed explanation of all aspects of excavation and trenching.
http://www.osha.gov/Publications/osha2226.pdf

Fall Protection in Construction
OSHA Publication 3146 (Revised 1998), 177 KB PDF, 43 pages.
http://www.osha.gov/Publications/osha3146.pdf

Occupational Safety and Health Administration

Ground-Fault Protection on Construction Sites
OSHA Publication 3007 (Revised 1998), 100 KB PDF, 31 pages.
Booklet on ground-fault circuit interrupters for safe use of portable tools.
http://www.osha.gov/Publications/osha3007.pdf

Lead in Construction
OSHA Publication 3142 (Revised 2003), 610 KB PDF, 38 pages.
Describes hazards and safe work practices concerning lead.
http://www.osha.gov/Publications/osha3142.pdf

OSHA Assistance for the Residential Construction Industry
Many OSHA standards apply to residential construction for the prevention of possible fatalities. This web page provides information about those standards and the hazards present in residential construction. It was developed in cooperation with the National Association of Home Builders (NAHB) as part of the OSHA-NAHB Alliance.
http://www.osha.gov/SLTC/residential/index.html

Selected Construction Regulations (SCOR) for the Home Building Industry (29 CFR 1926)
OSHA Publication (Revised 1997), 1.2 MB PDF, 224 pages.
Provides information on safe and healthful work practices for residential construction employers; identifies OSHA standards applicable to hazards found at worksites in the residential construction industry.
http://www.osha.gov/Publications/scor1926.pdf

Stairways and Ladders
OSHA Publication 3124 (Revised 2003), 155 KB PDF, 15 pages.
Explains OSHA requirements for stairways and ladders.
http://www.osha.gov/Publications/osha3124.pdf

OSHA
Occupational Safety and Health Administration

Working Safely in Trenches
OSHA Publication 3243 (2005), 2 pages.
Provides safety tips for workers in trenches. A Spanish version is on the reverse side.
http://www.osha.gov/Publications/trench/trench_safety_tips_card.pdf

Crane Safety

Safety and Health Topics: Crane, Derrick and Hoist Safety -- Hazards and Possible Solutions
December 2003. One page.
OSHA website index provides references to aid in identifying crane, derrick and hoist hazards in the workplace.
http://www.osha.gov/SLTC/cranehoistsafety/recognition.html

Electrical Hazards

Control of Hazardous Energy (Lockout/Tagout)
OSHA Publication 3120 (Revised 2002), 174 KB PDF, 45 pages.
This booklet presents OSHA's general requirements for controlling hazardous energy during service or maintenance of machines or equipment.
http://www.osha.gov/Publications/osha3120.pdf

Controlling Electrical Hazards
OSHA Publication 3075 (Revised 2002), 349 KB PDF, 71 pages.
This publication provides an overview of basic electrical safety on the job.
http://www.osha.gov/Publications/osha3075.pdf

Safety and Health Topics: Lockout/Tagout
OSHA website index to information about lockout/tagout, including hazard recognition, compliance, standards and directives, Review Commission and Administrative Law Judge Decisions, standard interpretations and compliance letters, compliance assistance and training.
http://www.osha.gov/SLTC/controlhazardousenergy/index.html

Hazard Communication

Hazard Communication: Foundation of Workplace Chemical Safety Programs
OSHA website index for resources on hazard communication.
http://www.osha.gov/SLTC/hazardcommunications/index.html

Frequently Asked Questions for Hazard Communication
OSHA, 6 pages.
Website questions and answers on hazard communication.
http://www.osha.gov/html/faq-hazcom.html

Hazard Communication Standard
OSHA Fact Sheet No. 93-26 (1993), 3 pages.
Highlights protections under OSHA's Hazard Communication standard.
http://www.osha.gov/pls/oshaweb/owadisp.show_document?p_table=FACT_SHEETS&p_id=151

Hazard Communication Guidelines for Compliance
OSHA Publication 3111 (2000), 112 KB PDF, 33 pages.
This document aids employers in understanding the Hazard Communication standard and in implementing a hazard communication program.
http://www.osha.gov/Publications/osha3111.pdf

Chemical Hazard Communication
OSHA Publication 3084 (1998), 248 KB PDF, 31 pages.
This booklet answers several basic questions about chemical hazard communication.
http://www.osha.gov/Publications/osha3084.pdf

NIOSH Pocket Guide to Chemical Hazards
Handy source of general industrial hygiene information on several hundred chemicals/classes for workers, employers and occupational health professionals.
http://www.cdc.gov/niosh/npg/npg.html

Material Handling

Materials Handling and Storage
OSHA Publication 2236 (Revised 2002), 559 KB PDF, 40 pages.
A comprehensive guide to hazards and safe work practices in handling materials.
http://www.osha.gov/Publications/osha2236.pdf

Personal Protective Equipment

Personal Protective Equipment
OSHA Publication 3155 (2003), 305 KB PDF, 44 pages.
Discusses equipment most commonly used for protection for the head, including eyes and face and the torso, arms, hands, and feet. The use of equipment to protect against life-threatening hazards is also discussed.
http://www.osha.gov/Publications/OSHA3155/osha3155.html

Safety and Health Topics: Personal Protective Equipment
OSHA website index to hazard recognition, control and training related to personal protective equipment. http://www.osha.gov/SLTC/personalprotectiveequipment/index.html

Toxic Metals: Cadmium

Safety and Health Topics: Cadmium
OSHA website index to recognition, evaluation, control, compliance and training related to Cadmium.
http://www.osha.gov/SLTC/cadmium/index.html

Electronic Construction Resources

OSHA eTools and Expert Advisors can be found on OSHA's website: http://www.osha.gov

eTools

Construction: Preventing Fatalities. Construction can be a safe occupation when workers are aware of the hazards, and an effective safety

and health program is used. This eTool will help workers identify and control the hazards that commonly cause the most serious construction injuries. A Spanish translation of this eTool is also available.

Scaffolding: Supported Scaffolds and Suspended Scaffolds. These eTools provide illustrated examples of safe scaffolding use. Hazards are identified as well as the controls that keep those hazards from becoming tragedies.

Solutions for Electrical Contractors. This eTool describes common hazards that electrical contractors may encounter and possible solutions for these hazards. The eTool was developed in cooperation with the Independent Electrical Contractors (IEC) as part of the OSHA-IEC Alliance.

Steel Erection. America's 56,000 steel erectors suffer 35 fatal accidents per year, a rate of one death per 1,600 workers. OSHA estimates that 30 of those deaths as well as nearly 1,150 annual lost-workday injuries can be averted by compliance with provisions of the Steel Erection standard, developed with industry and labor through negotiated rulemaking. To that end, this eTool has been created to educate employers and workers.

OSHA's Expert Advisors

The Asbestos Advisor: This computer program provides an introduction to the scope and logic of the regulations for general industry, construction and maritime.

Lead in Construction Advisor: This computer program provides an introduction to the scope and logic of the regulations regarding occupational exposure to lead and summary guidance to facilitate compliance.

Occupational Safety and Health Administration

Construction Industry Cooperative and State Programs

Voluntary Protection Programs

OSHA recognizes Voluntary Protection Programs (VPP) worksites for their excellent safety and health management systems.

OSHA Construction

OSHA has announced an OSHA Construction program to address the unique needs of the industry. The goal of this program is to make VPP more accessible to construction employers, especially small construction employers and to maintain the high standards of VPP while expanding participation to broad construction industry categories such as short-term projects, mobile workforces, general contractors and subcontractors. Pilot programs in these categories have shown beneficial results for participants.

OSHA Challenge

OSHA has created the Challenge Pilot to provide greater opportunities to eligible employers interested in working with OSHA to create safer and healthier workplaces. The pilot is designed to reach and guide employers and companies in all major industry groups who are strongly committed to improving their safety and health management systems and interested in pursuing recognition in VPP. OSHA Challenge provides participants a guide or roadmap to improve performance and ultimately the opportunity to take part in the VPP Merit or Star programs.

Alliance Program

Alliances enable organizations committed to workplace safety and health to collaborate with OSHA to prevent injuries and illnesses in the workplace.

OSHA has a number of national and regional or area office alliances that impact the construction industries. The details of these alliances can be found on www.osha.gov under Alliances.

OSHA Strategic Partnership Program

Partnerships are voluntary, cooperative relationships between OSHA and groups of employers, employees and employee representatives (sometimes including other stakeholders and sometimes involving only one employer) that encourage, assist and recognize efforts to eliminate serious hazards and achieve a high level of worker safety and health. National construction partnerships include AMEC Construction, Associated Builders and Contractors (ABC) and the National Ready-Mixed Concrete Association. In addition to the national partnerships, OSHA has had nearly 170 regional strategic partnerships with the construction industry since the program's start in 1998.

State Programs

Twenty-six States and territories operate their own occupational safety and health programs under plans approved by Federal OSHA. Twenty-two of these programs cover both private sector and public (State and local government) employees; four cover public employees only. States may have somewhat different requirements and procedures for the construction industry, but they are required to be at least as effective as Federal OSHA. All State Plans offer a VPP program and have additional cooperative programs parallel to OSHA's Alliance and Strategic Partnership programs. A list of States with approved plans may be found at www.osha.gov

Consultation

Every state offers a free, on-site consultation program to help small employers find and fix hazards and establish effective safety and health management systems. Funded primarily by OSHA, consultation is provided at no cost to small employers and is delivered by state authorities through professional safety and health consultants. More information on OSHA's Consultation Program appears on the agency's website at www.osha.gov

WORKER SAFETY SERIES

Success Stories

Partnership Reduced Injuries during Art Museum Renovation

In 2002, OSHA and AMEC Construction developed a partnership to prevent injuries at the $425 million rebuilding/renovation construction project for New York City's renowned Museum of Modern Art (MoMA).

The partnership covered some 220 employees and 17 employers who worked to more than double MoMA's space and expand facilities for special exhibitions, public programs, educational outreach and scholarly research.

AMEC employees completed more than 800,000 hours in 2003 and racked up two impressive safety and health statistics: the number of Days Away Restricted and Transferred (DART) percentage was 90 percent below the national average for their standard industrial classification (SIC) code and the Total Case Incident Rate (TCIR)

OSHA
Occupational Safety and Health Administration

was 92 percent below the national average for their SIC.

Best practices used included daily safety inspections conducted at the site and any hazards identified were corrected immediately. Inspection results were discussed at safety committee meetings. Each employee knew that a safety issue would be dealt with promptly when it came to management's attention. Additionally, an on-site incentive encouraged safe workplace practices.

The right combination of best safety management practices, partnering between OSHA and AMEC Construction, and a DART percentage 90 percent below the national average are fitting achievements for a new and better home for the world's leading collection of modern and contemporary art.

Fatalities Prevented, Injuries Minor, Workers' Comp Costs Slashed

Turner Construction and OSHA Teamed Up on Wisconsin Stadium Project

Teamwork at the Green Bay Packers' Lambeau Field is not just for professional football players. A partnership between Turner Construction and OSHA made teamwork in achieving health and safety a top priority for construction workers building and expanding the stadium.

In 2003, the $295 million renovation of the Lambeau Field stadium was completed, more than doubling the size of the previous stadium. Seating capacity was increased from 60,890 to over 72,000.

Partnering with OSHA paid off. There were fewer serious injuries for workers and a more than 20 percent cut in workers' compensation costs for the contractor.

The partnership had three goals:

- All contractors have an effective safety and health program;
- All hazards corrected daily after daily audits are conducted; and
- Increase the level of training for supervisors and employees.

The work was more hazardous than typical steel erections because stadiums are curved and angular in shape. Also, construction and demolition activities were taking place simultaneously, often within a few feet of each other.

Several potential serious accidents were avoided by requiring all contractors' safety and health programs to establish a requirement of 100 percent fall protection at or above six feet.

One worker on the project slipped off a steel beam located six stories above ground. Thanks to his use of full fall protection, serious injury -- or possible death -- was avoided. He was back at work shortly after his rescue. Less than two months later, a second worker slipped from a beam, but also escaped injury because of his fall protection equipment. Like his coworker, he returned to work the same day. An ironworker and a carpenter also fell and were saved by their harnesses.

CONSTRUCTION 33

A significant achievement included 4,300 workers completing OSHA's 10-hour construction training. An added benefit for the industry is that these employees are bringing their safety training to other sites where they are now working.

OSHA
Occupational Safety and Health Administration

OSHA
Occupational Safety and Health Administration
U.S. Department of Labor
www.osha.gov

Employers are responsible for providing a safe and healthful workplace for their employees. OSHA's role is to assure the safety and health of America's workers by setting and enforcing standards; providing training, outreach and education; establishing partnerships; and encouraging continual improvement in workplace safety and health.

This informational booklet provides a general overview of a particular topic related to OSHA standards. It does not alter or determine compliance responsibilities in OSHA standards or the *Occupational Safety and Health Act of 1970*. Because interpretations and enforcement policy may change over time, you should consult current OSHA administrative interpretations and decisions by the Occupational Safety and Health Review Commission and the Courts for additional guidance on OSHA compliance requirements.

This publication is in the public domain and may be reproduced, fully or partially, without permission. Source credit is requested but not required.

This information is available to sensory impaired individuals upon request. Voice phone: (202) 693-1999; teletypewriter (TTY) number: (877) 889-5627.

Made in the USA
Columbia, SC
25 April 2025